STOP PROCRASTINATING NOW!

10 Simple & SUCCESSFUL Steps for Student Success

august john hoffman

California State University Northridge
Compton College

julie nicole wallach

PEARSON
Prentice
Hall

Upper Saddle River, New Jersey
Columbus, Ohio

Library of Congress Cataloging in Publication Data

Hoffman, August John.

  Stop procrastinating now! : 10 simple & successful steps for student success / August John Hoffman and Julie Nicole Wallach. -- 1st ed.

    p. cm.

  ISBN 0-13-513056-5 (alk. paper)

  1. College students--Time management. 2. Study skills. 3. Procrastination. I. Wallach, Julie Nicole. II. Title.

  LB2395.4.H63 2009

  378.1'70281--dc22

                    2007036150

Vice President and Executive Publisher: Jeffery W. Johnston
Executive Editor: Sande Johnson
Editorial Assistant: Lynda Cramer
Project Manager: Kerry J. Rubadue
Design Coordinator: Diane C. Lorenzo
Operations Specialist: Susan Hannahs
Managing Editor: Pamela D. Bennett
Director of Marketing: Quinn Perkson
Marketing Manager: Amy Judd
Marketing Coordinator: Brian Mounts

This book was printed and bound by Bind-Rite Graphics. The cover was printed by Phoenix Color Corporation.

Pearson Education Ltd.
Pearson Education Singapore Pte. Ltd.
Pearson Education Canada, Ltd.
Pearson Education—Japan

Pearson Education Australia Pty. Limited
Pearson Education North Asia Ltd.
Pearson Educación de Mexico, S.A. de C.V.
Pearson Education Malaysia Pte. Ltd.

10 9 8 7 6 5 4 3 2 1
ISBN 13: 978-0-13-513056-8
ISBN 10:   0-13-513056-5

"Never do today what can be put off until tomorrow."

- Humphrey Bogart in *The African Queen*

# ACKNOWLEDGMENTS

This book is dedicated to the life and inspirational work of UCLA Graduate School of Education Professor James E. Bruno (12/12/40 – 07/11/06). Professor Bruno published hundreds of articles and books addressing the subjective experiences of time, school reform, and technology-based evaluations used to measure student achievement in higher education. His work and friendship to me have been highly influential both in my personal life and in my own scholarly research. Professor Bruno was the antithesis of procrastination and valued time spent with his family, friends, and students.

The completion of this text would have been virtually impossible without the support, patience, and encouragement I received from my wife, Nancy, and our two children, AJ and Sara. I would like to thank Executive Editor Sande Johnson for her patience and assistance in the inception of this book, with the editorial help of Lynda Cramer. Kerry Rubadue and Pam Bennett in production provided an in-depth editorial critique, which fine-tuned the final manuscript. My long time assistant and personal editor Julie Wallach contributed valuable assistance and insightful comments throughout the writing of this book and my thanks go out to her. Finally, I wish to thank my students who have always given me rich information and ideas for future work, and who actually inspired me to write a book about turning in assignments on time and avoiding procrastination. The following Pepperdine University students provided me with a *student perspective* in understanding and writing a book about procrastination: Ms. Kelly Willerding, Ms. Amanpreet Kaur, Ms. Krystle Madrid and Ms. Stephanie Pratt – Thank You!

I also want to thank the following reviewers: Michael Jensen, Utah Valley State College; Andrea M. Cole, University of Maine; Jill Hughes, Casper College; Jeanine Long, Southwest Georgia Technical College; Kaye Young, Jamestown Community College.

August John Hoffman, PhD

 # INTRODUCTION

How we experience and value time tremendously influences how productive we are throughout our lives and defines the quality of our relationships with others. The common phrases "Time is money" or "I'll meet you if I have time" or "Where did the time go today?" are all examples of the precious commodity of time, but more importantly, of how we have learned to misuse or devalue the importance of time in our relationships with others. When we wisely organize our lives, we can accomplish more and generally can improve the overall quality of our personal and professional lives. It becomes even more critical that we organize time efficiently as responsibilities and projects increasingly impact our lives. A poorly-organized lifestyle often results in the tendency to delay projects, which results in inferior or substandard work. Many individuals feel compelled to procrastinate as a means to *find extra time*. If you take the *time* to read this book carefully (and we hope that you do!) we can show you simple and effective skills to improve the quality of your professional and personal life by learning how not to procrastinate.

Why is it that you never seem to have enough time for the very important things in life? Do you really allow yourself enough time to experience important events or are you trying to do more and more in shorter blocks of time? Is it possible to accomplish your goals? And, how often have you identified an important goal that you know you need to accomplish, but you find yourself delaying this task until it is too late to complete? These are some of the prevailing questions that many people ask themselves when they habitually arrive late to school, delay projects or term papers, and then never seem to have enough time to spend with family and friends. Procrastination has become an increasingly more visible problem in our society as people delay more and more events in an effort to accomplish more in limited periods of time. Time, of course, has remained fixed (i.e., there will always be 24 hours in a day) but our schedules, and how we experience time, are necessarily more fluid.

There are many books claiming to help people achieve their goals through a variety of *self-help* techniques and time management skills. Malls, grocery stores, libraries, and even the Internet are replete with *quick-fix* mentalities as the best ways to get what you want out of life and cure your problems. This *fix-it quick* culture suggests that a simple and easy solution will be readily available if and when we need it. Therefore, we tend to wait for simple solutions to complex problems, becoming vulnerable to exploitation through manufacturers claiming *immediate results*. This strategy will not work; we must incorporate long-term changes into our lives to see long-term results.

Our approach in this book is different. Here we evaluate what procrastination is and provide solutions that you can use for the rest of your life. Overcoming the urge to procrastinate is often more about developing effective organizational and time management skills than doing less in a specified amount of time. All people have the capacity to overcome the problem of procrastination, but some remain unaware of their personal power and available resources in preventing it. People typically procrastinate because they are waiting for *the right time* or they simply do not know how to begin a particular project. They may fear the project itself or they may be disorganized in their approach to project completion or goal attainment. However, the longer they wait to begin the project, the less time they have to finish it. The less time they have to finish the project, the more anxiety they experience, and the cycle continues.

Advances in technology and a belief that *more is better* can also contribute to procrastination. Technology was supposed to be our modern-day cure for doing more in less time, a panacea for helping with tasks we had a hard time completing because they were labor-intensive or time-consuming. The inventions of the cell phone, the fax machine, the automated dishwasher (*ad infinitum*) were all supposed to give us more time and make our lives more comfortable and relaxed. However, has this really been the case? For example, cell phones typically mean more people can reach you just about anywhere (including the bathroom!) for unimportant or irrelevant calls, which ultimately means that you have less time to do what you want or need to do. The true irony of modern technology is that most of us have actually *lost* time by not controlling our use of technology. The key to avoiding procrastination is not through relying on technology, but rather through understanding better what our goals are and how to use technology and other tools to help us manage our time so we may achieve these goals. We have provided a summary in 10 simple steps for doing just that–what we call the **SUCCESSFUL Technique in Eliminating Procrastination:**

S	**Stay** *Focused on Goals*
U	**Understand** *Procrastination*
C	**Clarify** *Your Goals*
C	**Create** *Contracts*
E	**Educate** *Yourself*
S	**Support** *Systems*
S	**Simplicity**
F	**Find** *Your Strengths*
U	**Understand** *Deadlines*
L	**Look** *to the Future*

Each technique is addressed in greater detail in chapter 3. We hope that the information in this book will help you to better organize your time and ultimately help you to achieve your goals.

August John Hoffman, PhD
Julie Wallach

CONTENTS

PART 1
The What, Where, and Why of Procrastination

What is Procrastination?

Where is Procrastination Likely to Occur?

Why Do Student Procrastinate? Seven Styles of Procrastination

WHAT IS PROCRASTINATION?

The term *procrastination* refers to the practice of delaying completion of any responsibility, project, or activity until it becomes too late to complete it in a satisfactory manner. Most experts agree that over 90% of college students engage in some form of procrastination, and 1 out of 4 procrastinate to the point that they fail and drop out of college (http://ubcounseling.buffalo.edu/stressprocrast.html).

How Can Procrastination Influence Me?

How many people do you know, including yourself, who barely have enough time to eat breakfast in the morning, get to work or school, or answer e-mails and phone calls? Before they barely begin, it is almost time to go home again! To make matters worse, many times the really *important* responsibilities still need to be addressed. If this scenario sounds familiar, it is because people are trying to do more in less time. The problem is that there will always be a fixed amount of time in any one day, and our ability to *do more with less* ultimately reaches a breaking point.

Procrastination can impact us in many ways. Students may not submit required assignments on time, office employees may turn in late reports, and children may learn behaviors that actually foster procrastination. People may procrastinate for a variety of reasons, but in the end, the result is the same: Work is not completed on time or with the desired quality. What is perhaps most frustrating to individuals who frequently procrastinate is that they typically **do** have the skills and traits to complete their work well and on time, but due to lack of time management and organizational skills, they tend to leave their work incomplete.

Learning how to avoid procrastination can help you in many valuable ways:
- ∞ *Academic and Educational Performance Reorganized!* First and foremost, procrastination robs students of precious time that will help them to succeed in their academic work. Once you have learned some of the basic principles to reorganize your time and to develop better structure, you will be able to identify and organize your time to achieve your academic goals.

- ∞ *Employment – Getting Ahead Faster!* Once you have learned how to avoid procrastination in your academic work, you will be able to use these skills at work. And, when you become more time efficient at work, you increase your chances for earning promotions.

- ∞ *Physical Health – Just Do It!* Perhaps one of the most frequent topics involving procrastination relates to physical health. Many individuals delay important health and exercise programs. This behavior not only prevents them from feeling and looking better, but also can result in serious, long-term health consequences. So, when you understand the dynamics of procrastination, you not only improve your levels of academic performance and employment, you additionally improve your opportunities for good physical health.

Before we go any further in this book, you need to evaluate your own tendency to procrastinate. Complete the Procrastination Quiz on the next page by scoring your self on each statement. Then check your score against the Procrastinator Types to discover where you currently stand. We will further describe the 7 different types of procrastinators following the questionnaire.

Procrastination Questionnaire
"Am I A Procrastinator?"

Answer each of the questions below. Score each answer with either:
1 = Absolutely Not True
2 = Somewhat Not True
3 = Not Sure / Don't Know
4 = Somewhat True
5 = Absolutely True

_____ a. When I start a project or task, I feel comfortable leaving it unfinished for a while.

_____ b. I usually tend to wait for the *last minute* before I start projects because I need the pressure to do well.

_____ c. Sometimes I like to ignore certain things that I need to do because they tend to go away by themselves.

_____ d. I believe that it is much better to wait and give yourself time to do things right rather than to just get started on something.

_____ e. I like to do things over and over until they are just perfect–anything less than that to me is unacceptable.

_____ f. Sometimes I get so overwhelmed with what needs to be done. I don't know where to start and cannot get started.

_____ g. I often tend to underestimate the kinds of things that need to get done as well as how much time it takes to complete a project.

_____ h. Usually no one is available (or willing) to help me when I get stuck on a problem and need to finish a project.

_____ i. If I don't begin a project, I am not that upset because usually someone will volunteer to help besides me.

_____ j. I believe that things usually have a way of working themselves out if we just leave things alone.

_____ k. I feel that it is better for people to take their time gradually with a project and delay it rather than running the risk of working too fast and making too many costly errors.

_____ l. When I work in group projects, I like to listen to what others have to say and usually wait until someone tells me what to do.

_____ m. If I get hungry while right in the middle of an important project, I usually eat first then try to finish whatever it was that I was working on.

_____ n. Sometimes when I am working on a project if I cannot make it *just perfect* then I feel like it isn't even worth completing.

_____ o. I often feel that people get too *worked up* or anxious over things like due dates and time constraints. I believe that things always tend to work out for the better

_____ p. Sometimes it is better to leave things undone for a while until you know for sure that you are doing something right.

_____ q. People who establish goals in their lives are really setting themselves up for failure.

_____ r. I tend to avoid making commitments out of fear of breaking them.

_____ s. I tend to wait to do the most important things last. I know myself and that I tend to work better under pressure.

_____ t. Sometimes I think that it is better not to try something new just to avoid failing at something.

_____ u. My teacher at school (or supervisor at work) often tells me to try to get my work in on time.

_____ v. Often I am late to many activities and family parties because I can't seem to get started during the day.

_____ w. Often I plan many activities to get done on the weekend, but it seems that I never have enough time to get to them.

_____ x. I consider myself to be an impulsive person. Planning and organization seems to take the fun out of doing things.

_____ y. For the most part, I believe we actually can control few things in our lives. If it is *meant to be*, then it will happen.

Scoring: Now add up all of your scores and identify what type of procrastinator you are:

125 – 100: The *Type A* Chronic Procrastinator.
99 - 75: The *Type B* - Moderate Procrastinator.
74 - 50: Occasional Procrastinator.
49 – 25: Task Achiever.

Type A Chronic Procrastinator: 0% to 25 % of Projects Completed

The chronic procrastinator is someone who consistently delays or avoids meeting deadlines and commitments. The chronic procrastinator often is competitive and tense because he has not accomplished his goals. Important projects are seldom completed because the chronic procrastinator has incorporated procrastination into many projects in his life. He often engages in a type of self-fulfilling prophecy—he knows how important it is to complete a project successfully, and so he becomes preoccupied with minor details that then continue to delay progress and eventual completion of the project. An obsession with minute details also prohibits a chronic procrastinator from understanding the overall scope or purpose of his projects, which impacts his ability to achieve his goals. Often the chronic procrastinator also is a perfectionist—projects never get done because he never considers them good enough to consider final. Sometimes this perfectionistic behavior is an unconscious attempt to conceal his fear of failure. The irony of the chronic procrastinator's situation is that while he often is governed by his need for control, inevitably he relinquishes that control by delaying work on a project until the last minute.

Type B Moderate Procrastinator: 25 % to 50% of Projects Completed

The moderate procrastinator is unable to achieve his goals or meet his deadlines, but he typically is happy and shows few signs of stress. Where the *Type A* chronic procrastinator may not achieve goals due to perfectionistic tendencies, the *Type B* moderate procrastinator does not achieve goals because he simply is not committed to completing the tasks required to meet the desired goals. This category of procrastinator typically represents an individual who is more focused on having fun, enjoying himself, and disregarding responsibility. The *Type B* procrastinator typically represents the college student who would rather see a movie with his friends than study for an exam to be given the following day. The *Type B* procrastinator typically has the skills and aptitudes to achieve his goals, but a fear of failure tends to hamper movement toward goal completion. It is easier to say he failed at a project or an exam because he kept putting it off or didn't really try hard rather than to accept failure despite hard work, planning, and effort.

Occasional Procrastinator: 50% to 75% of Projects Completed

The occasional procrastinator shows the most promise in overcoming procrastination. An occasional procrastinator typically starts projects on time and completes the vast majority of them. However, this type of procrastinator often leaves a small amount of work incomplete and thus always has something left to do or finishes at a level beneath his aptitude. With just a little support and structure, occasional procrastinators may easily overcome this habit. The occasional procrastinator can often complete projects but lacks structure and organization in his routine. The occasional procrastinator can reach goals more successfully by implementing more structure as well as using self-help tools. This book focuses on the use of structure and self-help tools to overcome procrastination.

Task Achiever: 100 % of Projects Completed
Mission Accomplished!

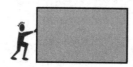

The task achiever is someone who rarely, if ever, procrastinates. The task achiever implements excellent time management skills and knows how to organize his time effectively. In addition, the task achiever also knows how to prioritize what needs to be done first, second, and so on. The task achiever realizes her limitations and therefore avoids taking on too many projects at the same time. He is usually quite effective in group projects and can help people take a team-oriented approach to completing projects. A task achiever learns how to maximize his time wisely and complete projects on time; but, more importantly, if the task achiever knows that he cannot complete an important task on time, he uses a support network and makes arrangements to get the task done. A task achiever does not ask for more time, which is simply an extended form of procrastination.

My Personal Wish List

The purpose of this book is not necessarily to show you how to do more in less time (*although we will review some important time-saving tips*); but instead, the purpose of this resource is to show you *how* to *avoid* procrastinating altogether. The key is to become more organized with your time so you can accomplish the important things in your life. Disorganization may be only *part* of your procrastination problem. As you will see, there are many factors associated with procrastination. But let's be clear---procrastination *steals time from us* and compounds the problem of time management, which keeps us from achieving our goals.

To some degree we all procrastinate. Many of us have specific goals but have not yet achieved them due to procrastination. Some of these goals may include a higher grade point average, better time-management skills, starting a regular exercise program, and so on. Now that you are aware of the level at which you procrastinate, the next step is to identify those goals that you have not yet achieved because of it. Below list 3 current goals that you have not achieved due to procrastination:

My Personal Wish List: 3 Current Goals I Have Not Yet Achieved

1.

_____

_____

2.

_____

_____

3.

_____

_____

Now ask yourself why you have not achieved these goals. Perhaps you might say that your time is limited and that you never seem to be able to get around to doing the important things in your life. There may be some truth to how busy your schedule is, which is the reason that organization is critical to reducing procrastination. The better organized and structured your daily routine is, the less likely you will fall into the procrastination trap.

Procrastination and the ability to achieve goals are foremost concerns in our daily lives. Technology and increased responsibilities greatly impact us all, making our capacity to organize and manage time critical tools in achieving our goals. One important factor that promotes procrastination is a naive belief that we can control events in our world in order to help achieve our goals. When external events interfere with our ability to control a situation, we relinquish personal responsibility in the outcome. As a result, we may adopt behaviors that promote procrastination. Holding yourself accountable for your actions and committing to the behaviors necessary to achieve your goals are two important components in improving your performance at work or school.

A second component of procrastination involves decision-making and specific goal identification. We often know what we need to do and how to do it. Perhaps we need to improve our study skills or improve the quality of our work, but we may never actually do it. Knowing what needs to be done and how to do it but choosing not to complete the task creates a debilitating sense of frustration and low self-esteem. Once we find ourselves in this state, it is easier to be distracted from our goals by every option from leisure activities and recreational programs to technological devices.

If we do not maintain focus and structure, we are easily sidetracked from our goals and then rationalize our behavior by creating excuses for not completing our tasks and goals. A high volume of e-mail or text messages, urgent, unscheduled calls, faxes, and Internet activities easily distract us from completing our responsibilities. Modern technology is a double-edged sword, the advantage being that individuals and information are capable of reaching us faster and more often than ever before. However, the equal disadvantage is that technology has eroded the privacy we need to efficiently and effectively complete our tasks. The more we divert our attention from the tasks at hand, the more likely we are to procrastinate, hoping to create extra time to finish our work.

The problem is that we are never able to *catch up*, and thus, we feel compelled to procrastinate even more. Procrastination actually *prevents* us from completing tasks and realizing our true ability and potential. Once we begin the cycle of procrastination, it becomes difficult, if not impossible, to actually begin work. Many people know what they want. They even can map out the steps to get what they want. However, they often sabotage their own desires by putting off until tomorrow what could be done today.

Think for a moment about your own lifestyle and all of the goals that you have, both short term and long term. Now ask yourself just exactly how successful you have been in achieving those goals. Do you have the skills and capacity to achieve your goals? Below list some of your short-term and long-term goals and the skills that you need to achieve them.

My current short-term goals and skills needed to achieve them:

Short-Term Goal _____

Skills Needed to Achieve _____

Short-Term Goal _____

Skills Needed to Achieve _____

Short-Term Goal _____

Skills Needed to Achieve _____

My current long-term goals and skills needed to achieve them:

Long-Term Goal _____

Skills Needed to Achieve _____

Long-Term Goal _____

Skills Needed to Achieve _____

Long-Term Goal _____

Skills Needed to Achieve _____

The greatest threat to achievement rarely is the lack of ability, but rather a tendency to think that we can *put things off*. The most common result of this tendency is a person's failure to complete the task either on time or with sufficient quality.
Eventually, the questions become:

- ∞ At what point does procrastination become so problematic that it prevents us from achieving happiness and a sense of success in our lives?
- ∞ At what point does procrastination interfere with our potential to reach our highest academic, professional, and personal goals?

In addition to the perfectionistic tendency mentioned earlier, you might find yourself procrastinating due to fear of task completion, disorganization, or overcommitment. Overcommitment is one of the most common reasons that procrastination continues to be a problem for many people. Extending yourself beyond your reasonable limitations can make you feel overwhelmed and ultimately can result in an inability to complete even simple assignments. For example, students in college may enroll in several classes without realizing the need to structure their time appropriately, or an employee may take on too many assignments at work. In either case, if individuals do not structure their time appropriately to meet their responsibilities throughout the day, they begin to put things off and the work remains incomplete.

As we have seen, procrastination may manifest itself in a variety of ways. We might experience procrastination in our professional, social, and interpersonal lives. You might pass up an important promotion at work because you want to wait for a better opportunity. Unfortunately, the opportunity that you thought would always be there may cease to exist. As a student, you might pass up an opportunity to study with other students because you think a different group of students might be more helpful. However, that different group of students never gets organized enough to pull it together. As a result, your academic performance suffers. A friend of yours frequently passes up opportunities to socialize with new people because he assumes that the opportunity to meet *the right person* will always exist in the future, but ends up spending a lot of time alone. Procrastination affects all of us, and our lives can be negatively influenced as a result of our tendency to delay important goals that are actually within our reach. Interestingly, Solomon and Rothblum (1984) found in a survey among college students that over 65% wanted to learn ways to prevent delaying projects in school. This finding suggests that the majority of us struggle with issues related to procrastination.

Social and Cultural Influences that Perpetuate Procrastination: The Increase in Self-Entitlement Attitudes—Let Someone Else Do It!

Procrastination may also be influenced by cultural values and attitudes. Some cultures may not emphasize task completion as much as others, inadvertently allowing procrastination to manifest itself in other types of situations. In this section we will look specifically at a cultural phenomenon that appears to be positively correlated with procrastination: Self-entitlement.

Today our society is focused on individual freedom, achieving goals and getting the most out of life by achieving individual happiness. We strive for what Markus and Kitayama (1991) refer to as the *independent self-concept.* According to these researchers, the independent self-concept refers to an expectation that individuals in society should develop a self-concept that is distinct and independent from others. Interdependence within these cultures is discouraged, as autonomy and individual success and freedom are perceived as critical aspects of identity. American culture emphasizes individual happiness and independence from others. Living in a highly individualistic culture as is found in the United States, we tend to emphasize and value winning, competitiveness, and success which often occur at the expense of other people. We tend to focus on what the group or community can provide for us, rather than focusing on what we can do for society or the community. We reward children for *individual* success rather than personal sacrifices made for the collective group.

The individualistic culture emphasizes individual success and happiness at the expense of the group or community. Unfortunately, this type of culture does not always educate individuals about *how* to achieve their goals *individually and independently from the group*. Rather, it emphasizes the need to rely on the group to accomplish goals. People who live in an individualistic culture have become immersed in an "ends justify the means" philosophy, emphasizing individual autonomy at the expense of the group itself. The irony of living within the individualistic culture is that we still need to rely on the group for accomplishing many of our goals. The expectation of individual success at the expense of the group places us within an inherent paradox: Achieving individual success and personal autonomy requires group assistance.

For example, some in our culture encourage children and adolescents to engage in what is referred to as a *self-entitlement* relationship with others. As our tendency to depend on the group increases as a way to achieve individual success, *there is also an increasing trend to delay our goals (to procrastinate) because of our expectation for others to assist us in meeting them.* Self-entitlement actually exacerbates procrastination because it encourages an undue expectation to relay on others to help us complete our work. The more people delay in assuming individual responsibility, the more problematic procrastination becomes.

Take a moment to think about the following typical situations that occur frequently within our society. Let's begin with educational performance among students in our school system. If a child performs poorly in school, the initial reaction is to find a reason. Is the failure the fault of the educational system, faulty teaching skills, or an incompetent teacher? With increasing frequency, we tend to find the reasons for our failures within other people or situations rather than accepting responsibility for ourselves. We tend to blame others (i.e., teachers, parents, employers) and only as a last resort do we consider our role and responsibility in perpetuating the undesirable behaviors. This type of culture in which we refrain from assuming personal responsibility or even expect others to assume responsibility for our behaviors is referred to as a *self-entitlement* culture. The self-entitlement culture has played a key role in the prominence of procrastination that we see today. For example, when you expect others to do things that you yourself should be doing, you delay doing these projects yourself. When your children do poorly in school, you expect others to fix the problem rather than helping them take responsibility and action on their own.

This tendency to externalize responsibility for one's performance frequently extends into the school environment. Many times, it seems, students are not held responsible for their own academic performance. Students could learn early in their education how to plan and organize their work, as these are the key skills necessary for avoiding procrastination.

Another area impacted by externalizing our rationales for various behaviors is childhood obesity. What is the relationship between childhood obesity, procrastination, and the self-entitlement culture? When children and adolescents are taught to not accept personal responsibility for their eating habits and physical activity, they may learn to blame others for their own unhealthy condition. Parents may blame food manufacturers and fast food restaurants for producing *addictive* and unhealthy foods. On occasion, these parents have brought lawsuits that most often are discarded by the courts as *frivolous*. However, the trend is certainly disturbing and precedent-setting, and exemplifies a self-entitlement culture.

Quite evidently, our culture has embraced an increasing sense of self-entitlement. This increase in self-entitlement exacerbates procrastination because it allows people to avoid assuming personal responsibility. The problem with self-entitlement is that when we no longer assume personal or individual responsibility, we expect others to do things for us. When this happens, we delay the very tasks that we should be completing independently. The following graphic illustrates the direct positive correlation between self-entitlement and procrastination:

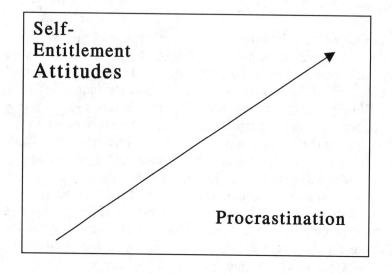

 # WHERE DOES PROCRASTINATION OCCUR?

We have described procrastination simply as a tendency to delay important projects. We have outlined ways that procrastination can result in serious consequences, in the professional environment, at school, and within our interpersonal relationships. Procrastination can occur any time that an important project or an assignment is due. We have identified four basic classifications of procrastination. In this section we will explore each type of procrastination and ask you to suggest ways to prevent it from reoccurring again in the future.

Employment Procrastination: Why Haven't You Gone Further in Your Career?

You have just arrived at work 20 minutes late and there are already 5 yellow stickers alerting you to address *urgent* tasks that need your attention today. Your phone rings and your secretary informs you that one of your clients is calling about a package that should have been delivered yesterday. Moreover, a client is waiting in your reception area to discuss an important account and you are already five minutes late for that appointment.
What do you do? Where do you begin? Write your response below.

_____

_____

_____

_____

_____

_____

Academic Procrastination: Improve Your Academic Success

You enter your biology classroom 10 minutes late because you missed your bus and your professor announces that a research paper will be due in one week. You already have one report due on that same day, and a math exam is scheduled for tomorrow. You have an appointment to participate in a study group later this afternoon and you are supposed to bring a summary of today's biology lecture.

What do you do? Where do you begin? Write your response below.

_____

_____

_____

_____

_____

_____

Interpersonal Procrastination: How Procrastination Influences Your Relationships with Others

You and your spouse enjoy going out to dinner and the theatre, and you have made plans to go to dinner and see a play that is showing one night only. Your employer contacts you at 4:30 in the afternoon that day and asks you to work overtime for an important project. This project is for a multimillion-dollar account and your work is critical to completing the project on time. Do you cancel your plans with your spouse to go out to dinner and see the play, refuse your supervisor's request and go out anyway, or take another action?

What do you do? Where do you begin? Write your response below.

_____

_____

_____

_____

_____

_____

Age-Related Characteristics and Procrastination: How it Affects All of Us in Different Ways

Childhood Procrastination:

Your 7-year-old son has a hard time getting out of bed on school mornings, and often misses his bus. Because of this, he is responsible for selecting his clothing for school the day before. I addition, he has the responsibility of keeping his room tidy, including taking dirty clothes to the laundry room. Your son has just received a computer for his birthday. You are happy that he has become proficient using the computer, but he spends so much time using it that you have had to help him get ready for school every day this week, and his dirty clothes are scattered on his bedroom floor. He has just arrived home and turns on his computer to show you a new skill he has learned. As a parent, how can you guide your son to not procrastinate while still fostering his interest in his new learning tool?

What do you do? Where do you begin? Write your response below.

_____
_____
_____
_____
_____
_____
_____
_____

Adolescent Procrastination:

Your 13-year-old daughter comes home from school and immediately sits down in front of the television. You have asked her several times to begin her homework, but she seems to put things off until the last minute. Her room is a mess, her homework is not done, yet she complains about "not having enough time to get things done." As a parent, what should be your response?

What do you do? Where do you begin? Write your response below.

_____
_____
_____
_____
_____
_____
_____
_____

Adulthood Procrastination:

You bought your first home a year ago. Before you moved in you had planned how you were going to decorate and use each room. However, after you moved in, you got distracted by work responsibilities and entertaining, so you have yet to unpack most of your boxes or finish decorating any room besides your living room. In addition, you seldom have time to read magazines and newspapers, sort mail, and so forth, so you have boxes of printed materials stacking up. Your closets are a mess, and you can't find clothes you know you own. You feel overwhelmed by the clutter and don't know how to start organizing. You even avoid going home because of the situation, spending a lot of time out with friends or working late. You feel something must change soon. *What do you do? Where do you begin? Write your response below.*

_____

_____

_____

_____

_____

_____

_____

WHY DO STUDENTS PROCRASTINATE? SEVEN STYLES OR TYPES OF PROCRASTINATION

- ∞ The *Perfectionist Procrastinator*
- ∞ The *Relax it Can Wait Procrastinator*
- ∞ The *Fantasizer*: Always Asking "What If?"
- ∞ The *Last Minute Procrastinator*
- ∞ The Anxious or *Fear of Success Procrastinator*
- ∞ The *Overambitious Procrastinator*
- ∞ The *Disorganized Procrastinator*

The *Perfectionist Procrastinator*: The Irony Between Perfectionism and Procrastination

At first glance, procrastination and perfectionism may appear to be the antithesis of each other. If anything, the perception about the *Perfectionist Procrastinator* is that projects are more likely to be completed *ahead* of time. But, as we saw earlier in this book, chronic procrastinators are often perfectionist at heart. The classic traits of a Type A procrastinator include competitiveness, hostility, and a sense of urgency to complete projects ahead of time. If anything, perfectionist (Type A) personality types often complete projects early or *before* deadlines. How, then, can they even be considered a type of procrastinator? The answer is in *how* the projects are completed by the *Perfectionist Procrastinator*. The *Perfectionist Procrastinator* has the compulsion and chronic need to keep revising, changing, or modifying projects to the point that they never are complete. Indeed, the *Perfectionist Procrastinator* may often take on challenges and responsibilities of other individuals, thereby making it virtually impossible to get anything done on time. Sometimes these individuals may engage in procrastination by trying too hard to do something *perfectly* as opposed to identifying a realistic result based on project guidelines and dates.

A project may be submitted early or on time, but the *Perfectionist Procrastinator* may revise and continue to *improve* projects well beyond their deadlines. Results are never quite good enough, and thus the need to change and improve them is constant. Just as in the metaphor of Sisyphus constantly attempting to push the boulder up the mountain and never being successful, the *Perfectionist Procrastinator* is often frustrated by his attempts to achieve perfection in his project or task. Unfortunately, the state of perfection can never be achieved, and thus the task is left incomplete.

Additionally, procrastination can be controlling. Perfectionists may want to *remain in control* and complete projects or begin activities on their own, independent of other people's assistance. Some may even take this behavioral tendency to an extreme and insist on doing everything *their own way*. Often the perfectionist procrastinates unintentionally by insisting on doing the bulk of work or completing projects independently, without the assistance of others.

Finally, the *Perfectionist Procrastinator* often has a deep fear of failure. It is far easier for the perfectionist to say "I did poorly on the project because I simply ran out of time" rather than saying "I finished the project, did my best, and still did poorly on it." In the first statement, the procrastinator implies that his ability to do the work exists, but that he simply ran out of time. However, the second statement suggests the lack of skill or ability. Acceptance of the notion that he might sometimes fall short of desired results can help a perfectionist to learn valuable lessons that could lead him to become more adaptive and successful. The *Perfectionist Procrastinator* should learn to allow others to participate in each project and set realistic standards when projects should be complete. At some point, the *Perfectionist Procrastinator* should be encouraged to say "We did our best" and accept whatever the outcome of that effort.

Strategies for the *Perfectionist Procrastinator*:
- ∞ Learn to recognize that *perfection* is a goal you can never achieve.
- ∞ Select time frames to work in and resist the temptation to extend those time frames.
- ∞ Adopt more realistic standards of performance and identify specific times and dates when work will be considered *complete* and submitted.
- ∞ Allow yourself no more than three revisions per project.
- ∞ Take time to relax. Structure time for work while also allowing time to relax between projects.

The *Relax, It Can Wait Procrastinator*

The irony of the *Relax, It Can Wait Procrastinator* is not in having too little time to complete projects, but rather in believing the misperception that he has plenty of time to complete a variety of projects. Thinking time will never run out, the *Relax, It Can Wait Procrastinator* never feels compelled to organize or structure his time. This type of procrastinator's relaxed approach to life dictates and determines how tasks get completed. He may feel that projects are not that important or that completing a project on time should not cause stress or worry. *Relax, It Can Wait Procrastinators* enjoy free time and seem to have difficulty organizing their time efficiently. If a project is due within one or two days, the *Relax, It Can Wait Procrastinator* may become easily distracted by a phone call or a visit from a friend and lose sight of his goal.

Strategies for the *Relax, It Can Wait Procrastinator*:
- ∞ Start all projects by writing down a in a short and to-the-point paragraph stating your goals.
- ∞ Write a contract to yourself promising to complete all tasks that will enable you to achieve your goals and become more cognizant of time. For example, write out a list for the week of the different kinds of things that you need to accomplish. Identify time slots and schedules in terms of where you are and what should be accomplished by a specific period of time. This will allow you to remain focused on time and time management skills.

The *Fantasizer Procrastinator*: Always Asking "What If?"

The third type of procrastinator, the *Fantasizer Procrastinator* often procrastinates because of ambitious (although unrealistic) dreams pertaining to his goals and thus seldom is able to begin the project. Fantasizer procrastinators often daydream about ways to improve their current projects, but unfortunately they lack such practical skills as selecting a day and time to actually begin the projects. To his credit, the *Fantasizer Procrastinator* has a tremendous amount of creativity and ambition. However, this ambition and creativity are never harnessed and structured in an efficient manner to allow these ideas to become reality. Individuals who find themselves often engaging in fantasy and asking themselves "What if this could happen?" need to embrace and protect their creative ideas while also focusing on becoming better organized. The *Fantasizer Procrastinator* needs to become more realistic with respect to turning ideas into a realistic vision through planning and structuring. For example, if the *Fantasizer Procrastinator* wanted to expand his ideas of a research paper into a broader and more global theme, he would first need to determine dates when his rough draft is due. Then he would hold himself to a long- term completion for the research paper.

Strategies for the *Fantasizer Procrastinator*:
- ∞ Identify more realistic goals that you can achieve. Ask yourself if your goals are concrete and tangible, or if they are unrealistic within the scope and timeframe of your project.
- ∞ Describe what your goals are to people who are close to you so that these people can encourage you to focus on your goals and support you in your efforts to achieve them.

The *Last Minute Procrastinator*

The *Last Minute Procrastinator* exhibits one of the more common types of procrastination. Often students may indicate that they have trouble beginning a project early because they need the pressure of a pending deadline to help motivate them. The problem with this thinking is that is that many of these students wait too long before they begin to study or write a paper, and by then, they have run out of time to do a quality job. The *Last Minute Procrastinator* often has the skills and the capacity to do good work, but when he begins an assignment, he runs out of time. Additionally, students may misjudge the time requirements of a particular project. The individual who procrastinates by waiting until the last minute is not using her time wisely and often mismanages her time in general by spending a lot of time on unproductive or recreational tasks. Typically the *Last Minute Procrastinator* will do almost anything to delay starting an assignment (for example, he has a ten-page term paper due Monday, but he practices golfing all day Sunday and starts his paper at 9:30 pm Sunday evening). Instead, the *Last Minute Procrastinator* should prioritize his projects based on importance and time management first, and then use what little time he has left over for leisure or recreational activities.

A second suggestion that has proven to be very successful with *Last Minute Procrastinators* is for them to make contracts or commitments. For example, if you know that you are the type to wait until the last minute to complete your work, you might make a contract with yourself to begin all important projects at least three days before they are due. If you are constantly late for work, appointments, or school, you are probably the type of person who tries to do too many things in a short amount of time. So, simply hoping that you will get to work or class on time in the future is inadequate and ineffective. You need to make major and significant changes in your life, such as getting an earlier start in the morning and ensuring that by a particular time you are in your car on your way to work or school, and then don't deviate from those guidelines.

Strategies for the *Last Minute Procrastinator*:
- ∞ Allow more time to begin working on projects.
- ∞ Create a schedule of your projects and goals, allowing for realistic estimates of time needed to complete each task. Adopt a 3:1 ratio when creating your schedule. In other words, for every project that you have identified with a specific due date, allow three days to prepare and complete that assignment. If a report is due on Friday, for example, you would begin working on that report on Tuesday.
- ∞ Make concrete changes in your time management that will positively impact your ability to get tasks done on time and avoid late arrivals to important events.

The Anxious or *Fear of Success Procrastinator*

The anxious or *Fear of Success Procrastinator* delays completing work not as a result of incompetence or lack of ability, but rather as a result of fear of what the future may hold after the project is complete. In many cases, graduate students who have been working on theses or dissertations for years may show significant fear in leaving their comfortable world of academia, thus prolonging the completion of their studies.

Strategies for the *Fear of Success Procrastinator*:
- ∞ Identify a clear future plan for yourself once your project is complete.
- ∞ Consult with family and friends and select three options for your career and future when you have completed your project. Identify what your choices and options are and then make a rational decision once your goals have been met.

The *Overambitious Procrastinator*

The *Overambitious Procrastinator* takes on too many responsibilities, making it impossible to complete the project or task. The *Overambitious Procrastinator* is typically the *workaholic* who finds meaning and satisfaction by taking on greater responsibilities relative to work or school assignments. These individuals often agree to perform work that far exceeds their capacity and are thus likely to require more time for completion. The *Overambitious Procrastinator* often is taken advantage of because of his willingness to do the work of others within the group. While this may seem to be an admirable quality, the disadvantage to is that often this type of procrastinator is not aware of his own limitations and puts the group at risk for submitting late or substandard work. The *Overambitious Procrastinator* often takes on an increasing amount of responsibility on a project, and then realizes that he has to delay the project because it is physically impossible to finish his tasks by the deadline.

Strategies for the *Overambitious Procrastinator*:
- ∞ Set realistic limits for what you can and cannot do in a limited period of time.
- ∞ Make a conscious effort to relax and to take time off from work as well as working towards your goals. Remember the importance of balance between what you do in work and leisure.
- ∞ Provide relatively equal amounts of work to each person assigned to each project.

The *Disorganized Procrastinator*

The *Disorganized Procrastinator* typically procrastinates due to a lack of structure and organizational skills. Tasks are not completed because there is no structure in the student's or employee's schedule. The *Disorganized Procrastinator* can be the most difficult to change because disorganization affects so many aspects of life.

Strategies for the *Disorganized Procrastinator*:
- ∞ Create a schedule that clearly organizes goals and responsibilities. Determine what is due first, second, and so on.
- ∞ Clearly outline in writing your project's requirements and resource you can call on if you need them. You might use a structure like the following:

Project Planner	MON	TUES	WED	THURS	FRI	SAT	SUN
What is due?							
When is it due?							
Who can help me?							

- ∞ Take the time to organize your workspace. Piles of papers scattered in random locations at your desk make it difficult to find what you need when you need it.

PART 2

10 Simple Steps in Eliminating Procrastination You Can Be S-U-C-C-E-S-S-F-U-L!

Stay Focused: What First Needs to be Done?

Understand Procrastination

Clarify Your Goals: What Needs to Be Done First?

Create Contracts for Yourself

Educate Yourself: Managing Complex Tasks

Support Systems - Take Advantage of Resources

Stay Simple - Know Your Boundaries: Avoid Peer Pressure

Find Your Strengths: What Do You Excel In?

Understand How to Work With Deadlines: Make Time Work For You – Not Against You

Look to the Future: Enjoying Your Life Without Procrastination

Future Tips: Preventing Procrastination Relapse

Staying Focused: What First Needs to be Done?

Identifying Goals

The single most important factor in eradicating procrastination is staying focused on your goals. The more clearly you have identified your goals, the more likely you will be to achieve them. Staying focused means first clearly identifying your goals and establishing a plan to achieve those goals *without becoming distracted or deterred.* Developing a plan that will allow you to achieve your goals is critical for successful task completion. The following is an example of how one student identified his goals and made a plan for achieving them.

List Three Goals Here and Identify Your Plan Strengths to Achieve Them

Goal #1: <u>Complete Biology report at school (3-5 pm); finish account at work.</u>
Goal #2: <u>Start exercising and get in shape. Lose 10 to 15 pounds.</u>
Goal #3: <u>Take time out once a week just to relax by myself.</u>

This student has listed three important goals that all deserve attention. But, which of the three deserves immediate attention and priority, second priority, and third priority? Goal #1 should have been his first choice, because a report at school or at work is critical to his status as a student or an employee (it is also something that typically cannot be delayed and has serious negative ramifications if it is submitted late). His second goal of exercising and losing weight also is critical and important; however, it can be implemented at his discretion in the future. The third goal, relaxation, also is important, but can be done at any time relative to his schedule.

Reschedule Your Schedule

As this previous example shows, once you establish goals, you need an organized plan to help meet those goals. That plan should clearly identify a time, place, and manner in which you will accomplish your goals. So, after you have identified each goal, you should next modify your schedule so that it is possible to achieve your goals. Are you the kind of person who is easily distracted? If so, commit to yourself that you will begin Goal #1 (for example, the Biology report or finishing an account at work from our previous example) at a specific time no matter what. Anticipate distractions (i.e., have cell phones turned off), shut your door to your dorm room or your office before you begin working. Allow yourself a minimum of 45 minutes before taking a break. Forty-five minutes of uninterrupted work time is like having three days of distracted work time. You will amaze yourself at what you can accomplish in 45 minutes of *quality work time.*

So, when establishing goals and scheduling your time to accomplish those goals, always ask yourself these questions:

o *When specifically* will you work towards your stated goals (i.e., from 9:30 am to 11:00 am)?

o *Where* will you work on your goals (i.e., the library, your office, etc.)?

o *What* is your target goal?

o *How* will you know if you have actually achieved your goal?

As a final suggestion, you may wish to identify environments that you find conducive to task completion. Identify those environments where you are more likely to stay focused and task oriented, such as the library or in the privacy of your own home, and avoid unnecessary distractions.

Understanding Procrastination

Fundamental attribution error is an interesting term in social psychology that describes the tendency to blame another person's behaviors on *dispositional* causes (he tripped because he must be clumsy) as opposed to the tendency to attribute our own behavior to *situational* factors (I tripped over something that was in my way). With the fundamental attribution error, we tend to view our behaviors as purposeful and organized but another person's as accidental or haphazard. Using this view, we are more likely to justify our own inability to reach deadlines whereas we tend to accuse others as being careless or disorganized when they fail to meet their deadlines. The phenomenon of the fundamental attribution error is important to our understanding of procrastination because it is one more way people rationalize their failure to complete projects on time. Furthermore, the fundamental attribution error demonstrates the inconsistency in how we view our own behavior as compared to other people's behaviors.

The fundamental attribution error should not be confused with internal or external attribution (a topic we discuss in the next paragraph). In the attribution theory, we simply make inferences about the types of things over which we feel that we have control. For example, with an internal attribution, individuals generally feel that they have more control over the outcomes of their behaviors. Conversely, with external attribution, individuals feel relatively helpless to control the outcomes of their behaviors and feel that their destinies are a matter of *fate* or chance. No one has an entirely internal or external attribution system, as these two systems tend to overlap. However, individuals who are chronic procrastinators often feel that their late or substandard projects result from circumstances beyond their control, thus placing them more in the external attribution category.

After reading the first part of this text, you may feel that you are not a procrastinator. Recall earlier that we said that all people procrastinate to varying degrees, So, becoming aware of your tendencies and patterns of procrastination is the first step to eliminating the practice. You might want to take a moment to revisit your responses to the procrastination questionnaire in the first section of this text.

Internal vs. External Attribution: What Types of Things Do We Actually Have Control Over in Our Lives?

Once you identify what type of procrastinator you are, you can identify what intervention methods are most effective for you. A common problem among chronic procrastinators is the tendency to believe they lack control over the important events in their lives, referred to as *external attribution*. So, it is especially important for the procrastinator to understand the principles of *internal attribution*, the belief that you actually have control over events in your life. *Attribution* is a term that was introduced by Weiner (1986) that refers to our perception of what we think that we have control over in our lives. For example, if you study very hard and earn an "A" on your exam, you probably feel that you had control over what grade you got. This perception is an internal attribution belief—you believe you have control over the grade you received. However, if you feel that no matter how hard you study for an exam you will still fail it, then this belief system is called an external attribution belief. People who feel that their lives are generally controlled by forces outside of themselves often feel that they are helpless to make positive changes in their lives. This helpless feeling tends to promote procrastination. Successful individuals typically feel that they have control over the majority of important events in their lives. They are realistic about what they can and cannot control, and they show an ability and willingness to learn from past mistakes so that they are not repeated.

An internal attribution (sometimes called *locus of control*) allows individuals to exercise control over positive and negative events in their lives and thus, they are typically happier and more productive because of this belief system. When individuals see several possible resources to help them accomplish a particular task, they know how to complete the project and they can exercise their autonomy in achieving their particular goal. Stated more simply, they have no need to delay a project because success is within their control. For example, students who have an internal attribution start out believing that they can perform well in school, improve their overall GPA through effective study skills, and establish positive relationships with others.

Students who believe that they have the power to control their learning and their grade performance are more likely to use resources to help achieve successful academic performance. Conversely, students who lack this perception are more likely to feel that their destiny is controlled and therefore refrain from using resources to improve academic performance. Significant research has been conducted, which illustrates that those who lack an internal attribution and feel that they are victims of fate and chance are significantly more likely to suffer from depression and unhappiness (Seligman, 1975). Furthermore, when people feel as though they are unable to control events in their lives, they are more prone to unhealthy coping mechanisms such as procrastination.

Developing an Internal Attribution System

How can individuals who procrastinate about various problems due to an external attribution change their perspective so that they actually feel capable of making positive changes in their lives to achieve their realistic goals? Remember, people who procrastinate generally do so because they have an incorrect perception of how events occur in their lives. They incorrectly feel that things *happen to* them and that they cannot *make things happen*. External attribution develops when we tell ourselves that our positive accomplishments have occurred simply as a result of chance or *fate*. Individuals who live with an external attribution fail to recognize their strengths, skills and aptitudes. *Thus, the first and primary factor in transitioning external attribution to internal attribution is in learning to take credit for things that you have accomplished.* Acknowledge and affirm your accomplishments on a daily basis, even if they are small.

A second important factor of developing an internal attribution is understanding the need to determine which events you have control over and which events you have no

direct control over. You choose how to spend your time. However, you do not control when assignments are due. Take credit for the activities that you successfully accomplished. For example, what have you done well recently? What do you love to do? What kinds of things provide *passion* in your life? Have you passed an important examination recently? Repaired an automobile? Consoled and communicated with someone who was depressed and thereby helped them feel better?
These are clearly actions that you *do* have control over. Recognize that they did not occur by accident or chance. If you harbor an external attribution, you tend to ignore the fact that your positive accomplishments are due to your own skills and aptitudes (controllable factors) and you probably attribute positive accomplishments to chance or luck. You also are likely to criticize yourself (i.e., "I'm just not good at doing those types of things.") and rarely take credit for your own achievements. Continually focusing on your real or imagined negative traits rather than focusing on your positive ones can lead to an external attribution in which you fail to understand that you have an ability to control positive outcomes and favorable events in your life.

When something negative happens to you that is *beyond our control* you can't be held responsible for the consequences, can you? However, you generally *do* have control over most events that occur in your life, both positive and negative ones. There are actually very few activities over which you ultimately do not have control. When you procrastinate, you might attempt to justify your behavior by claiming that the was due to *uncontrollable factors.* (You might say that your car broke down or that you were sick or that the teacher doesn't like you.)

When individuals are capable of recognizing those behaviors over which they have control and can identify several of their strengths and aptitudes, they are significantly less likely to procrastinate because they recognize that they have control over the outcome of important events in their lives. They do not fear making positive choices and decisions. Thus, learning the psychological dynamics of procrastination (such as understanding what we have control over or understanding our strengths and fears) are critical factors if we wish to truly overcome procrastination. In the following exercise, list successes and the internal attribution strategies you have used to achieve them.

Discovering Your Key to Success:
Internal Attribution

List three skills, aptitudes, or traits that you possess. For example, are you a good listener? A good communicator? Do you repair things readily? Are you a good cook? Are you able to work well with children?

1. _____
2. _____
3. _____

List three projects or activities that you completed by yourself and are proud of. For example, have you successfully completed a health program? finished your degree? gotten a promotion?

1. _____
2. _____
3. _____

Describe how you were able to achieve these successes. You finished your educational program, report, or earned a promotion by doing things that you had control over. For example, receiving a promotion at work typically occurs through consistent hard work, which you control.)

1. _____
2. _____
3. _____

Perhaps the single most important characteristic or personality attribute that is positively correlated with internal attribution is persistence, drive, and determination. Individuals with a strong internal attribution certainly are not successful in everything they try to accomplish. However, a consistent underlying theme of internal attribution is the *stick-to-it* attitude and determination that drives these people to keep trying until they are successful. Identify three goals that you have achieved through your own determination and perseverance.

1. _____
2. _____
3. _____

External Attribution and Procrastination: Why Bother Trying to Change if We Lack Control of Events in Our Lives?

If you feel that you lack the ability to control events in your life, you will likely avoid using the resources that exist to help you achieve your goals because you feel that they won't be of any use to you. Those who have an external attribution engage in negative self-talk, which further compounds a negative belief system about themselves. If you are one of these people, you might hear yourself thinking, I will never be any good at math so why should I bother even trying? Or, I will never get that promotion so why should I even bother trying? There is a strong correlation between external attribution and procrastination because when people feel that they lack control over important events occurring in their lives, they frequently delay them because they feel a negative outcome is inevitable regardless of their efforts.

Seligman (1975) discovered that individuals will usually stop trying to avoid negative conditions if repeated previous attempts failed. Suppose you are trying to lose weight but have been unsuccessful most of your life. Eventually, you will stop trying because you feel you are destined to be this way or you may defensively claim to others trying to help you, "This is how I am – deal with it." Similarly, if you feel that you have little control over the outcome of events, you will likely try to delay what you believe will be the inevitable outcome. So, you procrastinate! People who feel they are in a *hopeless situation* such as trying to complete a term paper at the last minute or *cram* for an examination do so because they dread what they perceive as an unavoidable negative situation. The more you tell yourself your efforts don't matter, the more likely you are to simply give up trying and accept the consequences. In Seligman's classic research with dogs, he exposed one group of dogs to a condition in which they received escapable electric shocks. A second group of dogs was exposed to a condition in which they were exposed to inescapable electric shocks. When the dogs were first exposed to the inescapable shock condition were transferred to a new escapable shock environment, they simply lay down and accepted the shocks without any effort to try to escape. Seligman generalized these results to humans in a variety of circumstances where repeated exposure to situations involving failure resulted in the humans simply giving up and accepting their conditions. For example, an individual who has tried to stop drinking alcohol in the past but has been unsuccessful might simply believe that it is impossible for him to stop abusing alcohol. A student who has repeatedly failed algebra in spite of studying and even working with a tutor, might believe that he is somehow genetically predisposed to fail in math, telling himself, that he is just no good at math . . . mathematicians are born, not made.

Once you see the link between external attribution and procrastination, improvement and change are right around the corner. When you realize that change is possible and that you control the ability to change, you will be less likely to procrastinate because you understand that your effort, organization, and planning can positively impact your outcome. For example, when an overweight person who develops internal attribution begins a diet and sees for the first time that it is possible to lose weight, he usually is highly enthusiastic because he feels success is possible and that he is in control of his destiny. Individuals who have experienced this process are much happier with themselves because they no longer need to procrastinate another diet or another term paper. The control and the power of success is now within their grasp.

Learning How to Control Important Events in Your Life by Reducing Procrastination

Learning internal attribution skills in many cases is as simple as actually *telling yourself* (and thus *believing yourself*) that success is possible. We call these positive thoughts *positive pep talks*. Routine positive pep talks help you gradually come to believe what you can succeed. Imagine the following scenario: You have studied very hard for an examination for over four days. You know that you fully comprehend the material and have mastered everything that you need to know to do well. You *know* this. You report to class, sit in your chair, but suddenly feel nervous or insecure. You begin to feel those familiar pangs of anxiety—and then it happens—you start telling yourself that you are going to fail even though you have worked so hard. Your palms get sweaty, you feel anxious, and you may even start to feel a little nauseated. Then you start to *psych yourself out* by thinking negative thoughts, such as *Why bother trying? The same old thing is going to happen. I get my hopes up and then get the exam back and have failed. Why even bother trying?* You can change this common negative thought process that is associated with external attribution by blocking out these negative thoughts and engaging in positive internal pep-talks, such as *I will do this* or *I know that I can do this* and *I feel good and confident and I am going to do well on this examination.*

With positive pep-talks, you tell yourself what you want to have happen and you are building confidence: *I have studied the material, I know the material, and I am going to get an 'A' on this examination. I may be a little nervous, but so are the other students in class. I am going to take my time, focus, and concentrate, and I will succeed.* With positive pep-talks, you are reversing the negative thoughts into positive thoughts that ultimately enable you to succeed and no longer procrastinate.

Developing internal attribution is based on three interrelated critical factors: determination, self-efficacy and persistence. Individuals with internal attribution systems all have one trait in common: they have the belief that if they just keep working at their goals eventually they will achieve them. Self-efficacy refers to the belief that you can achieve specific goals in your life. These goals are achieved typically by taking one step at a time, going slowly and gradually. As each step is mastered, your internal belief system is strengthened and your self-confidence and self-efficacy significantly increase. You can learn to change your external attribution system to an internal attribution system by remaining focused, determined, and committed. The following example illustrates the difference in how a negative external attribution system and a positive internal attribution system works for one student, Jim.

Scenario: Jim is a 20-year-old student who is trying to find balance between the demands of work, school, and his physical health. Jim is carrying a full load at school and does not have much free time for studying. Jim works overtime frequently and has a hard time trying to eat a healthy diet and participate in an exercise program at the gym. He has made several New Year's resolutions to lose weight, but by mid-February, the program has already failed. He is critical of his inability to maintain a healthier lifestyle, and is beginning to think that it really doesn't matter what he does to lose weight because the outcome is usually the same. His father and grandfather were also overweight and this further compounds his negative belief that he is predestined to remain overweight his entire life. We will now review Jim's situation from an external and an internal attribution system.

External Attribution (Negative Situation):
- ∞ Jim is an undergraduate student who is overweight and wants to drop 25 pounds
- ∞ Jim begins to procrastinate and delays his dieting and exercise program by telling himself, *I can start next month when I finish studying for this exam.* Jim continues to delay and procrastinate his health program to the point where he feels it is impossible to change.
- ∞ External attribution: *No matter what I do, I can't lose weight.*

   Result: Further procrastination of diet / no weight loss/ frustration

Internal Attribution (Positive Situation):
- ∞ Jim begins thinking positively and engages in positive pep-talks, such as: *I know I can lose weight if I just continue exercising and eat healthy foods.*
- ∞ Jim changes his external attribution (*I have no control over what I do*) to an internal attribution (*I can control what I eat and I can decide when to exercise.*). Most importantly, Jim's procrastination stops and he is actively involved in his diet and exercise program.
- ∞ Internal Attribution: *I control what I eat and how much I exercise. I know that fewer calories consumed than burned over time will result in weight loss.*

   Result: Gradual and successful weight loss. Jim no longer delays healthy eating habits and his exercise program. Jim is happy because he has increased his self-efficacy and self-esteem. He is more confident and now is back in control of his life.

Incorporating Positive Psychology as a Means of Achieving Your Goals

Positive psychology is a science related to what you *can* do, not what you are unable to do. It is a discipline that recognizes that all people are goal-oriented and capable of realizing their dreams, and asserts that the basis of most pathology rests in underachievement. It belongs to a branch of psychology that emphasizes our true potential by asserting that all individuals are unique and capable of making decisions within their lives for maximum growth. Positive psychology realizes that all persons are driven to become goal-oriented and are happiest when they are in the process of achieving their goals. The foundation of positive psychology lies in three principles:

- ∞ All people have more potential to achieve their *realistic* goals once they have identified those goals.
- ∞ All people have an inherent drive to exceed and excel and are achievement-oriented.

∞ Once a goal is achieved, the individual is more motivated to select future goals and is driven to become successful. Most people are initially unsuccessful in their drive to achieve goals because they do not know their true potential.

Three Key Factors in Positive Psychology

Cognitive:
- ∞ Optimism
- ∞ Internal attribution
- ∞ Self-Efficacy
- ∞ Positive and Optimistic Reframing of Thoughts (PORT)
- ∞

Physical:
- ∞ Increased aerobic/cardiovascular exercise
- ∞ Flexibility
- ∞ Outdoor Activity

Relational/Community:
- ∞ Increased interaction with other people.
- ∞ Opportunity to contribute and develop skills and aptitudes to the community

Three Key Threats to Positive Psychology

Procrastination:
- ∞ Postponing what you are capable of achieving

Hopelessness:
- ∞ Giving up on your self and others

External Attribution / Lack of determination:

Not assuming control over your destiny; for example, assuming that outside forces or events control your life and that you have very little influence over what happens to you.

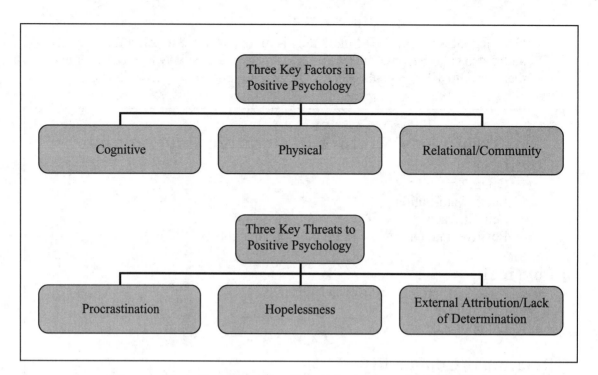

**Three Key Factors to Positive Psychology and
Three Threats to Positive Psychology**

Clarifying Your Goals: What Needs to Be Done First?

People procrastinate because they are unclear of the types about the goals that they need to accomplish to succeed in their lives, such as work-related projects, school assignments, and so on. When we can clarify our goals, we can develop a clear approach to understanding what needs to be done immediately and what can be done at a later time. Prioritizing is critical in any environment, and we will now offer some approaches for how to best prioritize to achieve your goals. The first approach is what we refer to as the *DONE* approach: Developing structure in your daily routine; Organizing your daily routine; Negotiating your goals; and Engaging in the task. Here's how to become more productive and efficient with your time by using the DONE approach.

Develop Structure in your Goals:

What exactly do you need to do first? Establish structure by identifying all of your goals and prioritizing what needs to be done first.

Organize Your Routine:

For example, if you have to work for three or four hours, then structure time so you may begin your project. Identify what project or task should be done first, second, third, and so on. Identify or label the degree of importance of each task, and be aware of the types of things that need your immediate attention.

Negotiate Your Goals Over a Particular Period of Time:

For example, if you have been procrastinating about completing a term paper for school, negotiate your terms. If you have one week left to finish your paper, then you can tell yourself that you can spend two hours a day on it for four or five days. Negotiating on your projects means identifying the best method to task achievement. For example, you have developed structure and have organized your activity levels. Let's say that you have a 10-page report that is due in three days. Negotiating the task means breaking it up into more manageable parts, say writing 3 pages on one night, 3 more the next night, and so on. Finally, negotiating your terms means that you entitle yourself to rewards when you complete your tasks.

Engage Yourself in the Activity - *Just Do It!*

At some point, all procrastinators must stop delaying and begin work, so make up your mind and just do it! Select a date and begin working, period. Perhaps one of the most critical components to overcoming procrastination, no matter how little you start on the first day, is to tell yourself that you have in fact begun the project. Remember, an important contributing factor to depression is continually putting off what we know we must do. The key factor in overcoming procrastination is getting started, no matter how small the progress, so you can tell yourself that it is a start and that you will continue until finished.

Develop - **O**rganize - **N**egotiate - **E**ngage

↓	↓	↓	↓
Structure:	Time	Goals	Activity
Prioritizing	*When* is it Due?	Identify Your	Do The Work:
Tasks: What	*What* Should Be	*Specific* Goals;	Avoid Distractions!
Needs to be	Done First?	how will these	Plan Rewards When
Done First?		Be Completed?	Done!

Create Contracts for Yourself

Contracts help reduce procrastination because they require you to set a firm date to complete a specific project. Usually there are negative consequences if the contract is violated. One highly effective method for controlling procrastination through improved organizational skills is to simply create a written contract for yourself where you list what goals need to be accomplished and the deadline for accomplishing them.

The Problem with Impulsivity – I Have Great Ideas but Never Complete Them

Highly impulsive individuals are those who appear to enjoy doing things *at the last minute*. Impulsive individuals are typically very spontaneous and are capable of changing plans at a moment's notice. Therein lies the problem. For all of the advantages of the creativity that impulsivity brings, there are also drawbacks. Often highly impulsive individuals are prone to procrastination because of their difficulty staying focused and completing required projects. If you tend to be impulsive, you need to remember to stay focused on specific goals until they have been completed. If you are highly creative, remain focused so you can effectively channel your effort and creativity towards task completion.

Writing contracts is a highly effective behavioral technique that allows you to clearly delineate and identify what your goals are and when they need to be completed. The advantages of the contract includes the fact that it clearly identifies what is due and when it is due. Additionally, effective contracts provide a list of rewards for meeting goals as well as sanctions for not meeting goals. For example, if you wrote a contract to complete an extensive term paper on time, you would not simply write *term paper due on Wednesday, June 10*. Rather, you would break it down into specific and measurable steps. Each time you complete a step, you receive an incentive to move to the next step.

Creating the Right Contract for You:
Identify *Your Goal* → **Create** *Your Contract* → **Finish** *Your Goal*

Contracts are highly recommended for individuals who procrastinate in starting and completing everything from academic assignments to health programs. On the following pages, we have provided you with a sample contract addressing three common problems: procrastination and academic work; procrastination and physical health; and procrastination and work.

3 Simple Steps in Creating a Contract to Improve Academic Work

Step #1: Identify the Goal and Purpose of this Contract:

complete research paper (list topic here _____)

Step #2: Create Contract for Achieving Goal – Identify the specifics of the project (i.e., When is it due? What is the length of paper? What are your goals in completing this project?)

Monday (5/30) = Abstract is due / consult with professor regarding paper topic

Monday (6/7) =   Introduction to paper is due

Monday (6/21) = First draft of paper is due

Monday (6/28) = Consult with professor or TA and review rough draft. How can your paper improve?

Step #3: Finish Goal

When you are able to see that you are making consistent and regular progress in achieving your goals, you are less likely to procrastinate and more likely to continue until successful completion of those goals. The basic idea is in structuring a realistic timetable so you know what you should be accomplishing in a relatively short period of time. The key component and most likely factor that causes procrastination is simply disorganization and lack of structure. Knowing what you need to do and when it needs to be done can be easily accomplished through the development of the contract.

3 Simple Steps in Creating a Contract to Improve Physical Health

Today many individuals are focused on having better health. Procrastination often is a major factor in preventing individuals from achieving optimum physical health. Something as simple as rearranging times to begin exercising may be all that is necessary to improve your physical health. Creating a *health contract* as a means of expediting improved health and preventing procrastination toward that goal may be the most important initiative that you can implement. Start by creating specific goals, as in the following contract.

Step #1: Identify Your Exact Goals. In many cases individuals who wish to improve their overall physical health have ambiguous goals (i.e., *I want to get healthy.*). Successful health programs typically incorporate contracts as a means of clearly identifying measurable goals (i.e., *I will lose 10 pounds, increase strength and stamina, reduce blood pressure, and report to the gym five days a week for 45 minutes under the supervision of a trainer.*)

Step #2: Create Contract in Achieving Goal

Step #3: Begin your health program based on the conditions that are stipulated in your personalized contract.
The following is a sample contract to improve physical health.

I, Ted Johnson, will make a commitment to report to the gym and work under the supervision of trainer Mary Smith for a period of time of one year. I will come to the gym at 7:00 a.m .for a minimum of three times a week (Monday, Wednesday, and Friday) and will participate in an aerobic or cardiovascular exercise program for at least 30 minutes, followed by a weight circuit of 20 minutes. Finally, I will complete my exercise program with at least 15 minutes of stretching and "warm down" exercises. Additionally, while participating in this exercise program, I have made a commitment to monitor my caloric intake and have been advised to use a low-carbohydrate diet recommended by my nutritionist. I will treat myself to a (non-food) reward for each week of successful participation, such as going to a movie, visiting my friends, or just making time for myself. I promise to faithfully adhere to these regulations, and if I violate any one of them (i.e., if I decide to sleep in one morning or if I eat the wrong foods), I will make a contribution of fifty dollars ($50.00) to any charity that Mary, my trainer, chooses each time I violate my contract. I have promised my health trainer as well as my family and friends to adhere to my decision to improve my health so they may also offer support to me. This program benefits and my famil and mey. Most importantly, I will make it a point each time I come to the gym to train to have fun, and to value and use my time wisely.

Signed: <u>Ted Johnson</u>

Witnessed: <u>Mary Smith</u>

Date: <u>Spring 2008</u>

3 Simple Steps in Creating a Contract to Move up the Corporate Ladder

Procrastination can occur at work and can prevent you from maximizing opportunities to advance your professional career. People within the corporate world often become complacent and may fall into an *employment rut* that can slow progress and even threaten their careers. People may have identified only general or vague goals without identifying specific procedures for how to achieve these goals. A contract at work will not only provide a timeline for you to make progress in your specific employment, but it will also help you to identify specific goals that may be necessary for you to get that promotion you have been wanting for some time.

Step #1: Communicate. First and foremost you need to communicate to your supervisor or employer what your intentions are. Where would you like to be in one year? Where would you like to be relative to your work in five years? Communicate to your supervisor and provide him or her with your ideas. What are some of the actions that you can take to help achieve your goals, such as attending workshops or continuing your education?

Step #2: Collaborate. After you have consulted with your employer, the next group to consult with would be your colleagues and co-workers. Collaborate with your colleagues to generate new ideas and strategies for meeting your employment goals. Identify what your ideas are and communicate these ideas with other workers to get as much information as possible. When you ask your colleagues about their views, they will generally appreciate the fact that you value their opinions and ideas. Additionally, collaboration with others will help you to maximize resources to achieve your goals in a timely and efficient manner.

Step #3: Create Your Contract. Create a personal schedule for your own progress at work that documents what your goals are. For example, instead of getting to work at 9:00 a.m., why not try getting into work earlier? Create a contract that details all of your goals and behaviors and identifies specifically what goals you wish to accomplish in a structured and specific amount of time. In six months or twelve months, what projects would you like to have completed? Have you taken the necessary precautions to maximize success? When you create a work contract, you specifically identify what goals you wish to accomplish in a specific amount of time. Many individuals at work have creative and original ideas that unfortunately are never realized. *These valuable and original ideas are never realized because the person thinking about them does not act on them.* Remember that when you actually identify and write down your specific goals in your contract, you are significantly more likely to achieve them.

*E**ducating Yourself:*
Managing Complex Tasks

Individuals often procrastinate in completing projects because they either do not have a clear idea of what they need to do or when it is due. Or they have created a highly negative and intimidating image in their minds that the project is either impossible or excessively difficult for them to complete by themselves. Usually, both of these perceptions are needless and inaccurate. Once the individual has accurately identified the scope and purpose of a project and outlined procedures for completing it, that project rarely maintains the negative and intimidating impact that it once had.

Some of the most successful techniques used to overcome procrastination involve basic behavioral techniques, whereby we simply break down complicated tasks into smaller, more readily achievable tasks. The process of dividing complex tasks into simpler and shorter tasks (followed by short rewards after each short task has been completed) is referred to as the process of *successive approximation* or shaping. The primary advantage of shaping is that it takes a complex procedure and simplifies it into a smaller, more manageable procedure to be completed at the individual's own personal pace. If we assume that a leading contributor to procrastination is a belief that the project is too large or overwhelming, then the logical solution to that problem is to break down complex projects into smaller and more manageable tasks.

How Shaping Helps Reduce Procrastination

There are two primary advantages when using shaping as a means to overcome procrastination. The primary advantage is psychologically-related. By breaking down larger projects into manageable steps, you are more likely to begin the project because it appears to be feasible. Once you begin a project, you will be more likely to finish it.

A second advantage in using shaping as an effective measure to reduce procrastination is that when we break down complex tasks into smaller and more manageable tasks, we are becoming more efficient and task-oriented in our use of time. As you may recall from the earlier part of the book, effective use of time through organizational skills is one of the most effective tools that you can use to reduce and ultimately eradicate procrastination.

For example, assume that an extensive research project or term paper is due in one of your classes and you only have one or two weeks to complete the task. You've been avoiding it, but now you know you have to start. Where do you begin? Shaping offers numerous advantages because it allows you to start with one small step and then because you know that you have actually begun the task, the intimidation gradually subsides.

The first step in creating an effective shaping task is to restructure the task into more manageable steps. If necessary, revise the project so it may be divided into smaller and easier tasks. The following shows an example of using shaping for a research paper project.

Sample of Shaping Program in Completing Research Paper

First: What is due? Define what exactly needs to be done and when it is due.

What is Due	Time Required to Complete	Completed?
10-Page Research Paper	One Week	No
a. Introduction Section	Two Days	No
b. Literature Review	Two Days	Yes
c. Procedure	One Day	Yes
d. Results Section	One Day	No
e. Discussion Section	One Day	No

Second: Create a shaping program that will allow you to complete your project on time.

a. Introduction Section: Two days to complete – I will finish on Monday, July 7, 2008;

Commonly Asked Questions:

How will I complete this task? I will go to the library and start writing the body section. *What are the resources that are available to me?* I can use the Internet and review similar studies and see how excellent papers are written. I can contact my professor and ask her advice on the topic. I also can contact other students and organize study groups and review sessions to compare my work with other students in the class.
Who can provide supervision so I know that I am doing this section correctly? I can contact the professor or the teacher assistant for the course, or I can consult other students in the class for information. I also can use the Internet and review articles with a similar topic so that I know that my format and technique in writing the paper is correct.

(After completing the shaping program for the body sections, detail the steps for completing the other sections in the paper)

Third: Create a short rewards system for following your shaping program.

What is Due	Time Required To Complete	Completed?	Reward:
a. Introduction Section	Two Days	Yes	Movies with Friends
b. Literature Review	Two Days	Yes	Dinner with Friends
c. Results Section.	One Day	Yes	Visit with Friends
d. Discussion Section	Three Days	Yes	Trip to Las Vegas

Why Offer Rewards in Shaping Programs? Shouldn't Completing the Project Be Its Own Reward?

The rewards system is very important for the shaping program as each successful accomplishment needs to be recognized and acknowledged with a small yet meaningful reward. When you begin to see that your work in small increments is making progress and that you are gradually taking positive steps toward achieving your goals, you need to be rewarded. Gradually the satisfaction of completing tasks in a timely manner will become the most effective reward. A further advantage to the shaping program is the simplicity that they can be implemented in just about any type of program .

Using Positive Psychology to Stop Procrastination: Restructuring Negative Thoughts into Positive Pep Talks

We have described some of the more common reasons people procrastinate. In many cases, procrastination may be a result of simply not organizing or managing time effectively, whereas in other cases, procrastination may include overambitious individuals who try to do too much in too short of time. A common third reason, related to the earlier discussion on attribution theory, is poor psychological skills. In many cases, individuals procrastinate because they are thinking inaccurate or negative thoughts that may contribute either to delaying the task or not completing the task at all. In other words, some individuals engage in negative or faulty psychological thought patterns that prevent them from achieving their goals because they have convinced themselves (inaccurately) that they cannot achieve their goals

Don't 'Psych' Yourself Out Before You Begin!

Positive thinking strategies are very effective techniques in helping people to achieve their goals. As mentioned earlier, positive pep-talks are very simple yet highly effective tools that help individuals to restructure their thoughts into a more positive and resilient perspective. This simple technique can facilitate successful task completion. Some people who procrastinate also view a project in a negative way, as something that *must be done* or as something that they will dislike. For many individuals, the reason procrastination even exists is because they have associated negative thoughts and attitudes with the project itself. These negative thoughts are often entirely false or at best exaggerated. With positive pep-talks, we can help reduce procrastination by allowing individuals to more accurately see positive characteristics that are associated with completing the project. Positive pep-talks also focus on the positive outcomes that the individual is capable of achieving rather than the negative outcomes for not doing a task on time.

Thus, instead of continuously repeating counterproductive thoughts that produce counterproductive results (i.e., "I'll never finish this report on time" or "I can't complete this amount of work in such a short period of time"), you should focus on more positive statements about completing projects. If you rehearse a series of different positive thought, such as *I know that I can do this* or *I will finish the first part of this report by next Tuesday*, you are not only telling yourself that you have the capacity to complete your work on time, you are also giving yourself structure in terms of when each project is due.

When we feel that we are capable of completing a project and when we have clear and realistic goals in turning in our work, we are significantly less likely to procrastinate.

The following are some examples of how to transition negative thoughts into positive pep-talks.

Work or School-Related Projects

Negative:
∞ *This work is too much for me to do by myself.*
∞ *I'm going to take some time off and maybe in a few days [or weeks] my attitude will change by itself.*
∞ *I'll never complete this project on time. Good mathematicians are born . . . not made.*
∞ *I am not good at this . . . and I won't ever be good at it.*
∞ *Maybe if I just ignore it for awhile, something will change by itself.*

Positive:
∞ *There is much to do in this project, but I know that I can accomplish it if I plan it outright and structure my time wisely.*
∞ *If I complete part one by today and tomorrow, part two by next week, and the last part within two weeks, I know that I can submit it by the required deadline.*
∞ *I like to excel in my work and I know that I have the capacity to learn and become even better at it.*

Health-Related Projects

Negative:

- ∞ *I have tried to diet and lose weight before. No matter what I do, it doesn't work. I may as well just give up and stop trying.*
- ∞ *I have always been overweight. It is impossible for me to change my weight and achieve a healthy and desirable weight.*
- ∞ *Most of my family members are overweight. I have a genetic predisposition to being overweight and therefore it is impossible to lose weight.*
- ∞ *I don't like gyms and I hate to exercise. I don't even know why I even bother to try to lose weight.*

Positive:

- ∞ *I know that it will be difficult but not impossible for me to lose 10 or 15 pounds. There are very few things that I cannot achieve if I put my mind to it.*
- ∞ *I know that if I plan things out and contact the right people to help me, I will be successful in my goal to lose weight.*
- ∞ *I am going to use all of the tools that are available to me, such as using a health trainer to help me develop an exercise program and a nutritionist to develop a healthy diet.*
- ∞ *I know that I can achieve my goal of attaining better health and losing weight if I select goals that are realistic and manageable.*

*S*upport Systems - Take Advantage of Resources

So often, we procrastinate because we feel overwhelmed and alone. You may not know whom to contact for help and support in times of crisis. Feeling alone and overwhelmed can often exacerbate the likelihood that a project or assignment will be late. In this section we will help you discover the vast assortment of resources available to help you complete your goals. You also may procrastinate because you feel you are surrounded by events that are beyond your control. When you have these feelings, you are more likely to feel frustrated and just give up. There are several viable resources that can be used to help you accomplish tasks. So often people who procrastinate need help but do not know where to find it.

One suggestion prior to beginning assignments is to mentally review your resources and potential to achieve your goals. The box *Discovering Your True Capabilities!* offers four simple steps to rehearse prior to beginning any project or task. When you feel more positive and *mentally recharged*, you are more likely to be successful in achieving your goals.

Discovering Your True Capabilities!

Identify Your Strengths:

Aptitudes, Skills, and Basic Talent. What Makes You Feel Good About Yourself? Develop Your Inner Positive Belief System:

Everyone Can Do This

Acknowledge Your Accomplishments:

What Have You Done That You Are Proud Of? How Were These Accomplishments Achieved? Recognize These Accomplishments Came from Your Skills, Not by Chance or Accident, but Through Behaviors That You Control.

Deciding on Your Future Goals - How Will You Achieve These Goals?:

Planning, Organizational Skills, and Support from Family and Friends. These Will Occur Not By Chance But Through Your Own Choices and Decisions.

Acting on Your Decisions. Goals are achieved when we realize we have the capacity and potential to acquire them and when we make the decision to achieve these goals:

Identify Your Goals and Achieve Your Goals Through the Use of Positive Pep-Talks. Tell Yourself
What You Want to Achieve and How You Will Achieve it.

Encouragement and Support from Family, Friends, and Mentors

Sometimes we are so entrenched in our own situation that we forget some of the most obvious places where we can turn for support. Often, support systems may be as close as the person next to us. Communicate your ideas, goals, and desires. Often just having emotional support can provide the impetus needed to actually achieve those goals. Just letting people know that you are beginning an important project or exercise program can improve your chances of completing the program because the support members might ask about your progress. When we know that others know about our goals, we feel more compelled to meet them. Simply knowing this may serve to motivate us to complete our projects once they have actually started.

Examples of positive and supportive networks that may help you achieve your goals are relative to the goal itself. For example, if you were interested in improving your health, you might consider hiring a health trainer to help you improve your health and fitness levels. Trainers not only provide valuable information to help you achieve your goals, but also often provide the support and encouragement necessary to succeed. You may also wish to tell your family and friends about your goals so they can provide support as you continue in your program. Perhaps having a training partner who knows that you have identified a clear goal and asking for his or her encouragement may be all that is necessary for success in achieving that goal. Whether you are a student who is using a tutor or mentor or a health trainer, these are all examples of how support is readily available and may prevent you from procrastinating on your path to goal completion. Other suggestions in using resources include:

∞ Teachers and professors often become instrumental figures in shaping our future. Often they even become mentors within our lives. Communicate with your teacher or professor about a particular course that historically has been problematic for you. Advise your professor that this class or assignment is very important to you and ask for ideas and suggestions relative to the course. This will not only improve your chances of academic success, but also will send the message to your professor that you are serious about doing well in that particular course.

∞ Employers and supervisors also can play a critical role in your future. They may serve as mentors if your working relationship is positive and motivating. Using your employer as a source for professional feedback about your career can be extremely helpful in the long run. Do not be afraid to ask for help from someone who has useful information that is critical to how your professional career could develop in the future.

Stay Simple - Know Your Boundaries: Avoid Peer Pressure

Know Your Limits and Avoid the *Just-a-Quick-Break* Trap

An important way to avoid procrastination is to know your own personal boundaries. In what situations do you work best? Are you an individual worker or someone who prefers working in a group? Procrastination often results when you select goals that are either unrealistic or impractical. If your goals become overwhelming, you are significantly more likely to resume procrastination and ultimately discontinue or abandon a project altogether. Selecting goals that are realistic and using support systems wherever possible are critical to enabling you to achieve your goals without procrastination. To illustrate the importance of identifying realistic goals, imagine this all too common scenario: A friend of yours has been frequently procrastinating about starting a diet and exercise program. He finally decides to act and begins dieting; however, his methods are unrealistic and even unsafe. He wishes to lose 50 pounds in *about one month* and has already become frustrated and is about ready to give up (again). What might you recommend to your friend?

First, recommend to your friend that he consult a health expert who can advise him in exercise, nutrition, and weight loss. Also recommend that he select a more realistic weight loss program. Losing 50 pounds in one month is unhealthy, unrealistic, and downright dangerous. Recommend to him that one year or more of consistent training and making positive and healthy changes in his lifestyle would be a more reasonable goal.

Second, you may want to recommend to your friend that he establish a reliable support network with his family and friends who can provide him with motivation and encouragement that he will need when situations get difficult. A positive support system will help your friend realize that he is making positive progress toward his goal and that he does in fact have control over his goals. With your assistance, your friend has now accomplished three key factors in the prevention of procrastination:

1. He has *identified his accomplishments* in weight loss and improving his physical health.
2. He has *made a decision to achieve his goals* and realizes that he has control over his actions and behaviors (i.e., engaging in exercise as opposed to watching television, or eating healthy foods instead of junk foods).
3. He is *acting on his goals* by making positive changes in his life (i.e., changing unhealthy lifestyles and behaviors, and established a positive and supportive network of family and friends).

Avoid the Trap of Peer Pressure: *Just One Break* or *Just a Quick Movie*

Often, well-meaning friends may interrupt you as you finally begin working on a project and may invite you out for a short break. Unfortunately, these short breaks often turn into hours, and when you do return from these breaks, your friends are gone, the hour is late, and you still have not finished your project. A key factor in preventing procrastination is in knowing your limits, establishing clear and structured goals, and learning to (politely) refuse potentially long interruptions in your work.

For example, if your goal is to complete a term paper or research project that is due very soon, you may need to take several short breaks in the process of achieving your goals. Your friends may offer to take you to dinner or a movie as a means of taking a *break*, but try to avoid the temptation. These *short breaks* often result in an inability to resume work, thereby prolonging your work and continuing the procrastination. Remaining structured and prioritizing your time are the key factors in reducing procrastination. Sometimes friends may not understand when no actually means no. Identify your goals within a realistic period of time and then reach them. Once these goals have been obtained, you once again will be free to spend your leisure time with your friends.

Finding Your Strengths:
What Do You Excel In?

Everyone has a variety of skills and talents that enable them to achieve their personal and professional goals. In many cases, however, people fail to acknowledge these strengths and simply focus on their perceived negative characteristics. Negative belief systems frequently increase the likelihood of procrastination because we naturally tend to delay what we perceive we cannot do. This form of a *negativity bias* becomes a self-fulfilling prophecy. Research suggests that the *negativity bias* has an interesting background and perhaps served an important need during human early evolutionary development (Ohman, Lundqvist, and Esteves, 2001). Being aware of potentially negative experiences or events, may have been an adaptive trait that allowed individuals to better address danger and protect themselves once they became aware of threats. Now, individuals are clearly more able to detect negative facial expressions, for example, than positive expressions, which can serve as a defense mechanism. Over time, this once potentially evolutionary adaptation, however, has become an influential force in procrastination and thus keeps us from completing the tasks at hand because we fear the anticipated negative outcome.

Conversely, people are naturally attracted to activities they are gifted in, and they are usually prone to complete these projects on time. When you identify skills and characteristics in which you excel, you can focus more on completing the project without risk of procrastination. If you engage in positive belief systems to help you achieve your goals, you will be more likely to complete a broader range of projects because you are motivated and have higher self-esteem.

Negative Belief Systems and Procrastination:
If You Think You Can – You Will

Have you ever realized that your thought process is inextricably linked to the outcome? Our behaviors often mimic what our thoughts are telling us. Think that it will be so, and it will be so. Often the best way to counter negative belief systems is in identifying those characteristics that you feel positive about. People who simply say that they are inherently inept or clumsy in a particular task exacerbate the likelihood of future negative behaviors, because they tell themselves to engage in negative behaviors to confirm their thoughts. The key to preventing a negative belief system from preventing your achievement is to simply counteract the negative thought with a positive thought or belief system. For example, what types of activities do you feel confident about and capable of completing? What do you naturally do well? What do you like about yourself? What types of activities do you do well in? Identify these topics and mentally rehearse them throughout the day. *You will discover that as you begin projects in which you excel and feel more confident about, you will also see a significant reduction in procrastination because you are doing something that you feel positive about and you want to complete.* Our next section will discuss specific techniques for identifying short-term realistic goals and how to structure your project and meet deadlines to help you achieve these goals.

Understand How to Work with Deadlines: Make Time Work for You, Not Against You

Typically, when people are told that they have a limited amount of time to complete a project, they become anxious and engage in negative thoughts such as, *It's impossible to do this in such a short period of time* or *I haven't been given enough notice to do the right type of work needed for this assignment.* Automatically, they engage in negative thinking. When this occurs they begin to set themselves up for failure. However, if they instead view deadlines as a tool designed to help achieve goals, and so as something positive, they usually will be able to finish their projects because they have defined the project's needs and deadlines. Therefore, deadlines should be viewed as a positive way to bring structure to a project to help us to reach our goals. Without establishing deadlines, we are unaware of how much work should be done in a limited amount of time, and thus we increase the likelihood of procrastination.

Establishing Effective Deadlines

In order to establish effective and realistic deadlines, you should go through a set of steps to help you think through the project.

- ∞ Analyze the project's needs. What is expected from me to complete this type of project? Do I have access to the tools needed to complete the project on time?
- ∞ Look ahead for potential problems or pitfalls. What could go wrong? How can you accommodate these potential problems?
- ∞ Identify your broad range of resources and support systems. Who can help you? Do you have experts available on the topic to contact (i.e., teachers, counselors)?
- ∞ Create a rough draft of the project.
- ∞ Critique, read, and review. When you are satisfied with it submit it. If you are not satisfied with it, continue the process.

Look to the Future: Enjoying Your Life without Procrastination

We have identified several factors contributing to procrastination. Mismanagement of time, disorganized lifestyles, lack of structure in one's own personal and professional life, fear of failure, and unrealistic perfectionist ideals can all influence us and set us up to procrastinate. The final recommendation of the *10 Simple Steps to Reduce Procrastination* will be in addressing methods to better organize your life so procrastination will not be necessary. When you look to the future you are planning ahead and becoming more organized. With proper organization, you can even plan for possible emergencies or other diversions and not be completely thrown off track when the unexpected occurs.

In this final section, we would like to identify skills and techniques that will help you prevent procrastination in future projects and activities. Perhaps as a psychological advantage, view your projects and assignments from a positive perspective. You are completing projects to show your strengths and skills, and thus viewing them as opportunities to learn and work with others. Assignments and projects actually afford you many opportunities to affirm your professional and personal strengths. They also provide wonderful opportunities to learn more about yourself (and others) and allow you to learn and experience self-growth in the process. The ability to engage in different activities without procrastination gives you tremendous potential to improve your self-worth, self-efficacy, and self-esteem. Thus, the psychological advantages of a procrastination-free lifestyle are numerous and can certainly add to the positive sense of well-being you deserve.

A positive perspective on task engagement sounds like this: *This project is an opportunity for me to show others the kinds of things that I love to do and do well.* A second possible positive psychological view might be: *Completing this project will allow me to meet people and learn more about myself. This is something I want to do.* The best way to experience your future without the negative influence of procrastination is through the conscious and rational development of a lifestyle that prevents procrastination from ever developing in the first place.

Future Tips:
Preventing Procrastination Relapse

You have just about learned about the *10 Successful Steps to Reduce Procrastination.* Hopefully, you have gained some valuable information about how we experience time and how procrastination can steal away valuable time that should be used to do the things that we need to accomplish. You might consider reading this book the first step that you can make in removing procrastination entirely from your life. Perhaps one of the most important points to remember in evaluating all of the intervention techniques that we have described begins with you making positive choices and decisions in your life. You, and only you, have the power to make constructive and healthy changes in your life. Engaging in procrastination and maintaining a disorganized lifestyle ultimately are choices that you can correct, provided you are aware of what needs to be changed. Remember this simple three part phrase:

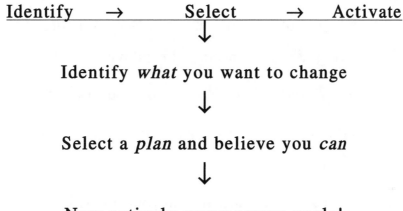

$$\text{Identify} \quad \rightarrow \quad \text{Select} \quad \rightarrow \quad \text{Activate}$$
$$\downarrow$$

Identify *what* you want to change
$$\downarrow$$

Select a *plan* and believe you *can*
$$\downarrow$$

Now actively *pursue* your goals!

We have reviewed several time-tested tips and suggestions to help you to better organize your personal and professional lifestyle without procrastination. In this final section we will summarize these techniques to help you improve your organizational skills and reduce procrastination. We also will provide you with some suggestions for how to actually do more in your life without procrastination. We also will briefly mention the topic of *relapse* to prepare you for the occasional *lapse* that comes with learning every new skill. All individuals, no matter how skilled or well trained, periodically experience what we call *relapses* or minor setbacks. We will show you how to use these minor setbacks to your advantage. Finally, we will offer you some brief suggestions that you may incorporate into your lifestyle to help you remain productive in your life and free from procrastination.

How to Do More with Less through N.O.I.S.E.

One of the more simple techniques used in preventing procrastination is the use of journals and logs that help individuals record their daily activities in a structured manner. Contained within these journals or logs are prioritizing systems that help remind you what types of things need to be done first, second, and so on. The single most important action that you can take in order to defeat procrastination is to develop a structured and organized lifestyle, doing what you actually have control over in your life (i.e., transitioning the external attribution system into the internal attribution system). Remember these five simple steps in the N.O.I.S.E. program to help reduce the likelihood of procrastination in future activities:

Now is the time to begin. Identify what you want to accomplish,

Organization: Increase your current **organizational levels.** What types of activities are due? Becoming organized means knowing **what** you need to do and **when** to do it.

Internal Attribution: Understand your own **internal attribution.** You decide and **you control** what you actually begin doing.

Structure: Increase structure in your life. **Increased structure** means not only knowing what to do, but when to do it.

Engage in the Task: Actually do the work. Your sense of accomplishment increases your task efficiency and decreases future procrastination.

```
┌─────────────────────────────────────────────────────────┐
│                  Now Achieve Your Goals                   │
│                           ↓                               │
│                     Organization                          │
│             (What needs to be done and when)              │
│                           ↓                               │
│                   Internal Attribution                    │
│        (Know that only you control what is being done)    │
│                           ↓                               │
│                       Structure                           │
│             (Know when it needs to be done)               │
│                           ↓                               │
│             Engage in the Task = Do It!                   │
│                  (Personal Fulfillment)                   │
└─────────────────────────────────────────────────────────┘
```

The Role of Modern Technology and Procrastination: Keep it Simple!

It is easy to walk into any electronics or department store and see the wide range of devices that exist purportedly to *help* us complete our daily activities. We generally become tempted with the vast array of equipment that can help us. The more obvious and traditional devices (such as the washing machine or the microwave) now seem unextraordinary given the vast assortment of computers, text messaging, and so on. Today, there are even many devices that clean and perform domestic chores, all in the name of saving us valuable time. The advertising for these products focuses on convincing consumers that the product will somehow save time and improve work efficiency. Remember, in the beginning of this book we described procrastination as a result of mismanagement of time and a lack of organizational skills. With the advent of the electronic age, it has become critical that we also learn to organize our information as well as our time. Electronic technology can only be as useful as our ability to organize time effectively, and many people mistakenly assume, when talking about information, that more is better.

Often electronic devices steal more time away from your schedule, which can cause you to procrastinate. Remember, people generally procrastinate not because they have too many things to do, but rather simply because they have not organized and structured their time wisely. Actually, individuals with packed schedules tend to know what they need to do within a limited timeframe and are usually successful in completing these tasks on time. If you own a lot of electronic equipment, gadgets, and devices, you may find that you spend much of your time maintaining this equipment. In essence these devices own you rather than you owning them. So we recommend keeping your use of technology simple, focused, and direct. The less complicated your lifestyle is (and the more organized you become), the more likely you are to complete your assignments on time. To illustrate how easily we can become distracted in our society, the average household in the United States owns approximately three televisions, usually one for each room and in many cases even one in the car. One wonders if devices such as televisions and cell phones are actually *promoting* procrastination by preventing us from focusing on more rewarding and fulfilling work.

Staying Focused Through Physical Exercise

A second way to avoid procrastination relapse is to maintain your physical health. Many students (and people in general) have forgotten how well a sound body influences rational and clear thinking. As a student, rational, clear, and logical thinking are prerequisites to completing outstanding research papers and engaging in intelligent thought. Exercise is an important and necessary activity that will help you remain focused and structured.

One might think that a positive correlation exists between the tendency to procrastinate and how packed one's calendar is. We would expect to find that the more we have to do in a limited amount of time, the greater the likelihood that we will procrastinate. This is not always the case. The more you need to accomplish in a limited amount of time, the more likely you might be to use the techniques discussed in this book. One strong recommendation is to achieve balance between your psychological and physical demands. As projects and workloads become increasingly intense and overwhelming, the need for balance and structure in our lives becomes increasingly important. An excellent technique that will facilitate balance in your busy schedule is maintaining a physical exercise program. Exercise and physical activity can help reduce procrastination by helping you to become more organized and resilient to stress.

Preventing Procrastination Through Organization: Know What to Do and When to Do It

As stated previously, many people procrastinate because they lack organization. Remaining organized may be as simple as creating a journal or log that identifies your tasks and when they are due (see the sample calendar in the appendix). Often many people complain that they get overwhelmed with too many things to do and are thus unable to complete projects at school or work. The best way for you to avoid being overwhelmed is to prevent it from happening in the first place. Prioritizing your tasks is a key component of organization. Developing priorities means completing what needs to be done first and knowing what needs to be done at later times.

- ∞ Prioritizing: What is most important and needs to be done now?
- ∞ Organizing: What are you capable of doing now?
- ∞ Executing: What schedule needs to be executed so that you can complete projects on time?

Concluding Thoughts: Maintaining Balance and a Healthy Lifestyle without Procrastination

Our final recommendation for maintaining your now procrastination- free lifestyle is to focus on balance between your work-related responsibilities, physical activities, and interpersonal and social needs. When you maintain balance, you will have a more productive lifestyle without the need to procrastinate. As a college professor, I have seen adaptive behaviors that have helped students excel during stressful periods (i.e., examinations), and I have seen students engage in maladaptive behaviors that have influenced procrastination. Typically, successful students are the ones who retain structure and balance in their lives and do not resort to ineffective behaviors which ultimately lead to procrastination. One of the key reasons they are capable of maintaining balance and structure in spite of the most challenging times is that they realize and have experienced the value of exercise in warding off stress. Conversely, those students who abandon their structured activities may "cram" for exams and actually perform more poorly on them.

Finally, if you concentrate on your studies and adequately prepare for your assignments and projects, you can improve the quality of your work without the negative impact of procrastination. In many cases, simply focusing on positive characteristics-- what you do well or what you feel especially competent about-- will have a positive influence on your ability to complete tasks well and on time. Emphasizing your personal attributes and strengths and maintaining positive attitudes with realistic goals will enhance your ability to live a *procrastination-free* lifestyle. These are the aspects of your life over which you ultimately have the control and power to change.

References

Bruno, J. E. (1997). *It's about time: Leading school reform in an era of time scarcity*. Corwin Press, Inc.

Markus, H. & Kitayama, S. (1991). Culture and the self: Implications for cognition, emotion, and motivation. *Psychological Review, 98*, 224-253.

Ohman, A., Lundqvist, D., & Esteves, F. (2001). The face in the crowd revisited: Threat advantage with schematic stimuli. *Journal of Personality and Social Psychology, 80,* 381-396.

Seligman, M. (1975). Helplessness: On depression, development, and death. San Fransisco: W. H. Freeman.

Solomon, L. J., & Rothblum, E. D. (1984). Academic procrastination: Frequency and cognitive-behavioral correlates. *Journal of Counseling Psychology, 31*, 503-509.

Academic Planner

The academic planner is critical in shaping your organizational skills. Organization, structure and balance are key factors that will lead you to success not only in your academic skills, but also in other important areas in your life. Identify what assignments or activities are due and list them (by month) on this handy calendar. Remember the three key factors to task completion:

What is Due? ✔ When is it Due? ✔ Begin Work !

Month _____

Sun	Mon	Tues	Wed	Thurs	Fri	Sat
		1	2	3	4	5
		*Decide Topic (5 Choices)		✔ Limit to 3 Choices		
6	7	8	9	10	11	12
		Identify Topic of Paper		✔ *Create Outline		
13	14	15	16	17	18	19
		*Create 1st Draft		✔ *Edit 1st Draft		
20	21	22	23	24	25	26
		✔ *Completed Final Draft				
27	28	29	30	31		

Glossary

Ailments: Physical or psychological problems affecting how we normally function (The patient's ailments were not life threatening).

Attribution (Internal / External): To assign a specific reason or particular cause (I attribute her reasons for behaving that way as being entirely egoistic.) Internal attribution: The belief that one has complete control over events incurring in one's life. External attribution: The belief that one has little (if any) control over events incurring in one's life.

Debilitating: Impeding progress; something real or imagined that blocks our ability to achieve our goals (The cold weather was debilitating to his recovery).

Deteriorate: To reduce in quality, substance, or value (The house began to deteriorate due to the inclement weather).

Exacerbate: To make worse or increase in intensity (The extreme heat exacerbated the patient's condition).

Learned Helplessness: The perception of an inability to change or improve one's condition (psychological or physical) despite having the resources to do so (The patient felt that his life would never change or improve despite pleas from his family and friends. His doctor indicated that this condition was symptomatic of learned helplessness).

Panacea: A cure for all problems or physical ailments (He believed that exercise was a panacea for all of his patients).

Procrastination: The practice or tendency of delaying or putting off the completion of any responsibility, project, or activity until it becomes too late to complete it in a satisfactory manner (The doctor told the overweight patient to stop procrastinating and to begin his exercise program).

Replete: Plenty to have; abundant or satiated (The pantry was replete with food supplies in case of any emergency).

Notes: